A Queen after God's Own Heart

Lakiethra Hardemon

Trilogy Christian Publishers
A Wholly Owned Subsidiary of Trinity Broadcasting Network
2442 Michelle Drive
Tustin, CA 92780

Copyright © 2021 by Lakiethra Hardemon

All Scripture quotations, unless otherwise noted, taken from THE HOLY BIBLE, NEW INTERNATIONAL VERSION®, NIV® Copyright © 1973, 1978, 1984, 2011 by Biblica, Inc.® Used by permission. All rights reserved worldwide.

Scripture quotations marked (KJV) taken from *The Holy Bible, King James Version*. Cambridge Edition: 1769.

All rights reserved, including the right to reproduce this book or portions thereof in any form whatsoever.

For information, address Trilogy Christian Publishing
Rights Department, 2442 Michelle Drive, Tustin, Ca 92780.
Trilogy Christian Publishing/ TBN and colophon are trademarks of Trinity Broadcasting Network.

For information about special discounts for bulk purchases, please contact Trilogy Christian Publishing.

Manufactured in the United States of America

Trilogy Disclaimer: The views and content expressed in this book are those of the author and may not necessarily reflect the views and doctrine of Trilogy Christian Publishing or the Trinity Broadcasting Network.

10 9 8 7 6 5 4 3 2 1

Library of Congress Cataloging-in-Publication Data is available.

ISBN 978-1-64773-880-8 (Print Book)
ISBN 978-1-64773-881-5 (ebook)

Contents

Modern Esther 5
Recovery 7
Sunflower 9
Notification 11
Reflection 13
The Fire 15
Forgiven 17
Faith 19
The Encounter 21
Control 23
What Gods Says 25
Patience 27
Divine Confirmation 29
Pray 31
Predestination 33
Change 35
Grace 37
Purpose Is Determined 39
Divine 41
Royal 43
Wants 45
Queens 47
Measures 49
Perception 51
Fruit 53
In the Midst Of 55
Partnership 57

VVS1 59
Game Changer 61
Salvation 63

Modern Esther

In the book of Esther, God shows us the beautiful love story of a very attractive orphan girl and the love that lay between her and a mighty king. In this love story, there was preparation, fasting, prayer, and tears—all the components of how to go before a king through God's eyes. But somehow, they did it all through love. In this story, it also presents doubt, deceit, and death. Within the hearts of God's people lies an Esther, and God is our King; He shows us how to talk to Him and get answers. In this we humble ourselves in the Lord and let Him renew in us a right spirit of excellence. We are no longer the orphan girl, but we become kings and queens after God's own heart, just like Esther took the heart of the king of Persia and did it diligently, and she was God's secret to get His people back in charge of a land that would set up their future of liberty. We are the modern Esther, and we are the secret that God wants to use in this millennium, to change the world. This is our purpose.

Recovery

Gotta learn how not to pick up the phone
Everything feels numb and new
I can feel this new person coming forth
Fresh smell and brand-new
It's crazy how a tragic hurt
Can make a person change in a matter of days
I felt like I had been through rehab for a few days
God had to remind me of who I was on so many levels
Pushed me to only care about Him and those who call Him Father
I started to exceed in my work and feel free again
Bondage is no place for any man
This recovery was a choice of an ethical life
The definition of choosing right over wrong in sight and out of sight
Repair me, O Lord, for my time is near
You took me and made me a queen beyond my years

Sunflower

With a central focus, sunflowers stay unified in purpose and position.
The definition of godly women.
The Bible says, "Behold, how good and how pleasant it is
For brethren to dwell together in unity" (Ps. 133:1)
And the world stops to see it!
For a sunflower gradually turns
Its most vulnerable scenery to the sun above,
All in unity to the most powerful source
Given from the God above, with creativity.
Rejoice, for the time is near;
Soak up the power source that God has given to His people,
For the greatest commandment is to love one another and pursue what is equal.
Build, mentor, and teach, for these are the instructions of a godly people.
Holy is His name, forever He reigns, over all the land.
Don't be deceitful and compromise His plan—
The devil comes to sift you as wheat and destroy identity,
For if you seek My heart, you will find your true unity within Me.

Notification

The buzz of the clock is a notification of time;
It doesn't stop time—don't waste time.
In this season time is so valuable,
Clock's ticking, Rapture around the corner.
God sends us notifications
In the form of prophecy, vision, dreams, and confirmation.
God's people know His voice.
God is roaring like a lion in the ears of His people,
To awaken them from slumber and fulfill His will.
Greater is He that is within me than he that is in the world.
Be not afraid, God can save.
But He needs willing vessels who are willing to endeavor
And get His people saved.
Sending notifications from sea to sea, country to country,
Oh, help our disbelief that God could really be preparing me for greater.
Awaken, Zion, and take your position.
God is with us, 2020 is just beginning.

Reflection

There is a way that God sees you,
Because He formed you.
There is a way others see you,
And there is a way you see yourself.
And from this point forward in your life,
It's going to depend through which mirror you are looking.
We compare ourselves to the things of this world
And count ourselves out because of our disbelief.
O God, create in me a clean heart
And make me to be more like You.
But compare ourselves to people who look more like God's opponent.
From wind to wind, I see and you see;
Change the hearts of those who seek you daily.
Becoming more like you means that they won't like me,
So if I find myself being too likable by those who don't strive to have meaning,
Produce change in me, O Lord, to press to be like You daily.
I refuse to conform to this dying world and risk not rejoicing in heaven for eternity.

The Fire

Glory, glory, to the name above
For God has sent a Holy Fire from above
It hit my soul and made my being come alive
God is the driver, and I was locked up for a ride
As praises flowed from my mouth
I was changing inside and out
I started to dance and sing with great triumph for my King
A burning fire within me to be what He wanted me to be
Holy, holy, the angels cry
So I started to mimic what I felt inside
Suddenly what was burning on the inside of me
Came out as a roaring lion
I was growing into what God specifically ordained for me
Created me in the sight of the Almighty
I look like my father
I dressed like my father
I talk like my father
I died to sin like my father
I had power like my father
I was guided by my father
Choose ye this day whom you want your father to be
I'm standing in the midst of God's glory

Forgiven

Stretched out in prayer
Reconciliation with Him
Making mistakes that I couldn't bear
Holding on to burdens felt no one cared
Dying from the inside out
So much so I experienced a drought
God listens to broken hearts
God hears a sinners prayer
So I decided to cry out, barely saying words of despair
He reached down and wiped my tears
Built me up and gave me wisdom beyond my years
Forgave my faults and restored the time in my life
Started me where I left off in Him
And gave me signs
I had now learned my lesson and was at peace
Only looking straight ahead in God's reasoning
Never know what the future holds when Christ is involved
I had nothing left, and God applauds
"Now I can deal with you
My daughter, you finally want Me"
Those words turned my life around
When I found out He was waiting on me
"Turn yourself from your wicked ways and pursue Me
I have more for you, daughter, talk to Me"
Healing began to take place, my heart was renewed
Emotional brokenness was healed too

Negative thoughts were replaced with scripture
I looked at myself in the mirror
And didn't recognize this picture
I physically look different to myself
I was changed, not the familiar

Faith

I go back and forth so much with God
Like, is it really gonna happen
Or is it just me
Sometimes I'm even waiting on Him
To give up on me because of my unbelief
My entrust, part of me keeps asking myself
"Why me" instead of "Why not me"
The insecurities show in me before my God
When He reveals His plan to me
He says, "You are prestige in the likeness of Me"
"Why not you, daughter
You reign in royalty
It's only right that you have the things
That I designed for thee
This is My will and this is My plan
Predestined to make the world
Go round and show My glory
This is not about you, this is about Me
Giving the knowledge to My people
So they can rest in Me
This is divine, I'm giving you signs
Now trust and believe
That what you ask is not too hard for Me
These desires I placed in your heart are Mine
Now set yours aside and walk with Me
You will stress yourself out doubting"

The Encounter

This is just the beginning,
The chills went up my back, and a dance in my feet
As I danced like David before the king
His power so strong I couldn't help but to praise
I went also into a weep, giving glory to His name
I craved the knowledge that His beauty portrays
I couldn't stop praying every single day
I sacrificed hours of sleep to call on His name
My soul cried out for Him to come speak with me and engage
The relationship between a father and his child
This relationship made my stress go down
What had I stepped into
When I started those twenty-one days of prayer
I was turning into another person
I discovered something new about myself every day
As I grew I felt this person in me come forth
She was bold, intuitive, and not bored
She spoke with authority and recognized her wrong
She strives to correct her life and all her wrongs
She apologizes
She encourages others
She cries for the dying
And God loves speaking to her
They speak like I'm speaking to you
No barriers in our way
This woman craves knowledge of the future

So she makes no mistakes
Her life is divine and arranged in and out of time
Demons flee when she awakes and calls on Jesus's name
This person is me, the person God wants me to be
God knew me before I knew myself
And now that I've stepped into it, I know who I am

Control

Here we go again
God loves to place me in situations that I have no control over
I ran through my head the things that bother me
Scared to empty these things
Because of accountability
Tears were rare to me
Sympathy grieved me
I lacked empathy, deceived me
I created this person self-made
In denial of my real feelings
I didn't have time to contemplate on what wasn't logical
Sustained by Grace
I was living in vain and blinded by a self-made personality
Control became an issue
Because I wanted everything in my hands
Not trying to gravitate to God's plans
Our human thought process can't comprehend the plans of God
So logic is not always the answer when faced with a problem
What happens when you need a miracle
Someone is on the deathbed
Logic will not be your friend
Only God can hold your hand

What Gods Says

What God says
God says I'm worthy
God says I'm extraordinary
God says yes
God is intense
God imprints deeply
God restored my soul
God made me whole
God gave you me
God speaks to me
God loves me
God never leaves me
God teaches me
God showed me
God blocked me
God says He will give me the desires of my heart
And I desire You
I press, I pray, I fast, I debate, that maybe I'm crazy
What made me look at you and decide to maneuver that way
Not even physically close to you
I wait, I wait, I prosper, I never faint to pray
I grow as God shows you little
But I did know he was preparing me for you
People pray for their significant others to be revealed to them
And don't understand the pressures ahead
Knowing who they are becomes a battle with the mindset

Instead to trust God and believe it will come to pass
It's what God says
He gave me priority and gave me a hand
So this is the goal, and I will get you to it
We will partner up, and I will show you how to wait for it
In our partnership, you don't have to worry about anyone but us
If you trust and believe in the God above
I am worthy, and I can make the impossible happen
Trust in Me, daughter of Zion
I am the way, the truth, and the light
And I speak life into a relationship that you never had planned
Partner with My son and glorify My name
He is a good leader, be blessed in Jesus's name

Patience

One of the hardest things to master
It was in my doubt that I realized what I lack
In grace I realized His love
In prayer I heard God's voice
In fear I learned the significance of faith
In this teaching I learned what imperfect was
Meltdown after meltdown
Tear after tear
Wondering if God was near and He was speaking clear
Frustration after situations
Prayer after prayer
Rest in Jehovah was my morning alarm in prayer
I took my heart and the things of it
And placed it in God's hands
I could not do it anymore
I found rest in knowing everything is predestined
Anything promised would come to me directly
No tricks, no schemes, just divinity
No steps before commuting
With God first, rebuke the enemy
For all I know
He is the only one who makes the final decision
I gave my life to Jesus's perfect tranquility

Divine Confirmation

With a sincere heart of knowing
I had already known what the answer would be
I took my lips and asked with desperation
Is he who I think he is
The one to be
A confirmation deep within me
An example of a love from Christ lived in me already
I carried part of Him and didn't know it
In the beginning He formed two
There was divine longing
I asked repeatedly this question
"You took my life and made it destined
My rib to be
In this I need Thee
I don't trust myself
Please help me"
God answers before we even finish the question
This was how I knew the answer was sent straight from heaven

Pray

When in prayer
You somehow feel like you are in between earth and heaven
No longer on earth
Lost in love as you ask for forgiveness
Personal time that you should put above all
Your mind is more powerful than any other muscle in the body
As you pray, you build from within
As He potters you
Prayer is significant to a change
It's the only thing that will keep you sane
When God's plan doesn't make sense
You speak from within
He gives you another language your enemies can't translate
And speaks through you what is hard for you to say
In the Bible God teaches of how to pray
He wants us to take a minute and call on His name
Simple conversation is what this portrays
Who doesn't want to conversate with royalty
And He loves you as well above all of what you call loyalty

Predestination

The will of the Lord is to come
I can feel my purpose drawing near
I have never experienced mind battles like these before
I struggle with casting my fears
I asked God, and He fulfilled
Yet I struggle to appeal my will
I never thought of myself as that important
Something had the view of myself so distorted
The devil on a rampage with negative thoughts
Trying to claim what he had lost
The tug-of-war going back and forth
What should I believe
Am I really the one
I ask that everything that is mine come forth
Started to pursue those things
Feels like I started a war
The war between flesh and spirit
Trying to differentiate which part of me is winning
I feed the spirit the devil hates
Touches my dreams while I'm asleep
Now I'm looking for a great escape
Don't be scared, trust in me, I hear
I've never left your side, my dear
A small whisper and a very gentle spirit
God was with me, and I could hear Him clearly
Dream after dream I was attacked

But knowing that in this means I was on the right track
Trying my best to change as God had already arranged my destiny
All I had to do was trust in God's predestination

Change

Some of the greatest things that God will do in your life will not be in your planner
When receiving a change
That you didn't have the faith to ask for is God's will
Asking for a change
Will not meet your expectations because He wants to exceed it
What you want for your life can't compare to God's mind
Or whether it's your season
You have to trust, have faith, to receive it
Change does not happen overnight
But it is a process
Having God as a life partner will give you heritage
Will give you favor
Will give you power and authority
Over the spiritual realm and the physical appeal
Stay in God's will
Change your routine and be intentional through these things
We all make mistakes
Stay diligent in all things

Grace

Deep in trouble
I was pulled from the abyss of my sin
A mighty, strong hand consumed me
As my spirit cried out from deep within
God lends us multiple ways of escape
And it's our choice to listen or decline
No matter what the devil hands you
There is always a design
He will hand you counterfeit things
That may seem right in the beginning
Until your soul starts to bleed
You start to drift and focus on vain things
The voice of the Lord becomes a whisper
A pressing to worship
In the service you start to feel different
Heavy, confused, and drifting into total silence
Unable to hear anyone but the negativity
Until that way of escape is your breakthrough
And you choose to accept grace
It fills you with a confidence that no one can replace

Purpose Is Determined

God's purpose will prevail
Mistake after mistake
Year after year
God's will was prevailing even when it was not clear
The vision may be blurry to us
But God knows the ending while you're still at the beginning
You may not feel worthy
You may feel trapped
You may feel insignificant
But God's will will bring you out
God's purpose and path may include the pit and the mountaintop
But have no doubt that God's will will bring you out
Many stray away because of dismay and disbelief
That God can take little old me and make me a queen
But God once told me, "I am a God of impossibility
Nothing surprises me"

Divine

I need answers
The bleeding of an aching push like no other
I can't stop
I won't stop dreaming
I won't stop believing
I've got to keep seeking
I have to keep worshipping
I have to keep praising
Even in the midst of the unknown
God is aware of the things that are in my heart
He prepares and He molds me into a star
If this is what you want, this is what you get
No turning back, no reprehending
It may seem hard, you may be tired
But this is the last push, do not retire
No looking back, my hands clutched tightly to my seat
As God takes us on a leap
This was my purpose, bright and clear
I brace myself, sweaty palms to my seat
As God smiles at me
Enjoy the ride, the time is near
The scenery beautiful, fond to me
I am in love with Christ
He is my eternity
Left flying in the air
Who knows what's in store for me

Royal

Heat on my back
Under attack
The longing for the outside
I can't relax
Waiting for my request
I've made them aware through prayer
I wonder if He can feel my spirit
O my sweet Lord, my dearest
The sweetest love story, my biggest
The longest enduring of my deepest thoughts and feelings
O God, I hope You feel me
It's past twenty-one days, and I'll keep going
All my life knowing you are in control
I behold, no time in my hands
I control nothing, I'm yielding to Your plans
Losing my mind, I give it over to the King
This must be what off earth feels like
You keep calling me
I'm losing my human being
I am not of this world
And the more I seek You
The more I feel like a stranger
Capture me with a desire for the love of a stranger
You seek, you find, I found you
Not on earth, somewhere in the middle of earth and heaven
I was curious, and I pursued

In too deep now to go back
Consistently under attack
Every part of me was too deep in to turn back
If I had attempted, I would have withdrawals like someone on crack
I could never leave, I could never stop praying
Craving the presence of my Lord, felt drunk daily
I was bleeding of sinfulness as He cleaned my soul to portray Him
My character, my personality, formed into an image like him
What was this transformation that I was experiencing
I had the ability to change things in the spiritual realm
It lay into a deeper calling
There were days when I would just look in the mirror
I looked physically different, no darkness
My complexion resembled an emerald

To be continued…

Wants

Beautiful songs intrigue me
You can't express wants
That you cannot feel deep within your being
It's unreal when it comes to you
A new dawn lights up in your understanding
A new warmth glows in your heart
A new power is given to your will
A new tenderness is given to your conscience
You've taught me so much and connected me to my future
You used perfect timing for me to truly seek You
My life is connecting on so many levels
You speak to me clearly
You have never left my side
You erased my pride
You called it done
I said "Amen"
You are the one

Queens

Fix the crown
Wipe the tears
Fix the eyebrows
In the bathroom stall with my head down
I reminisce on the things that bound me
My tears salty
A pity party draws me
But grace surrounded me and suffocated the negative things
I raised my head high
Stood with a sigh
And started to walk like I had Jesus inside
I heard the sound of my heels
Sounds like victory to my ears
Every click-clack appeals to the bravery revealed
Hope became real, the laughs, the zeal
The heart of a Queen preparing to master
Soft and strong
She walked out prepared to deal with anything that could go wrong

Measures

I'm faking it today, so can you please hold your comments
Something in me just was like no more
I can't take it
You have no idea of the feelings I'm feeling
Or the things that God has shown me
You have got to be pranking me
We have a measure of ourselves
God has a measure that exceeds our very thoughts
This world we live in today has its measurements as well
Measures of money
Measures of beauty
Measures of people that we know
Measures of education
We measure a lot
God even measures the level of our hearts
Sometimes we do it unknowingly
But this was shown to me
That this very thing does not compare to the plans God has for me
So I say faithfully, I believe in what God has put into me
That I can bear all things that God has placed in front of me

Perception

It's fine to see the good in people, but not just the good. We go every day meeting people who always wear mask. We thrive off pretending and fail to be ourselves. For those who have figured it out, only time will tell. In this world we live in, people hide behind books to cover up what the heart beats for but the mouth won't tell. They hide behind past anger and disappointment, which has furthered them from the truth that God still prevails. Even if you fought Him, He is still God. Even if you don't believe in Him, He is still God. Even if you read your books to get a better understanding of the color of your skin, God is still God, and hell is still hell, and condemnation is still condemnation. No matter how far you run from the truth, He still loves you and he will continue to pursue you. He is such a gentleman that He won't force you to take His hand, but He will wait until the day that you want to find out who He is.

Fruit

You can't expect fruit when you have planted rocks.
You reap what your product produces.
At the end, you can't be mad at anyone else if you fail a test or forget your lines.
You produced that outcome, whether you like it or not.
Evaluate yourself daily.
Check the ins and outs of what enters your eyes and ears.
Protect the mind and you protect the heart.
You produce your life.
This is just the start.

In the Midst Of

God comes in the midst of impossibility
Give Him a chance to be God so He can get the glory
The blessings we seek may not be in our reach
But God gives provision for us to call those things that we don't see to be
Many of God's people don't know what power lies inside our hearts
That's God's dwelling place, that cleans up what's deeply in our thoughts
We can be given insight about future events
Because our God holds the past, present, and future in His hands
So if worried about the things to come
Have faith, trust in Me, and have patience
That I am in control of every want and need
Beyond what you can ask or think
The battle is already won

—Lakiethra

Partnership

Partner with me, I'll show you who you are
My plan has always been to partner with My creation and show them My heart
I've planned the best for you, I've given you great thought
Love is intense, is unforgettable, and has a lot to do with the spirit
Connect to Me
Dwell with Me
Read about Me
Look to Me
I will show you greatness
Being in love in the spirit creates unlimited access
Walking in the spirit has no boundaries
It eliminates impossibility
This is what I intended for my people
Turn from your wicked ways and bow to Me

VVS1

VVS1 looks something like you and me
The definition of how we were built and described in God's eyes
The head and not the tail
The above and not beneath
Rich and not poor
Extraordinary and not ordinary
Peace and not destruction
Saved and not lost
Positive and not negative
Carefully made and divinely designed to succeed with an excepted outcome
Dipped in gold, a gracious people
Imperfect
Follower of the Creator
We look like Jesus the more every day
The truth is, we don't know who we are
Wake up and believe in who God says you are
The best, the salt of the earth, a worshipper, Judah
Hope—who are you?

Game Changer

He had given unto me a new walk
A new plan
A new development that I myself had not obtained in my mind
He consulted a preparation, a preparation of faith
Faith was the game changer
It changed my name
It changed my mindset
It changed my speech
It changed the reason I breathed
Faith is the believing without seeing
He told me my future and gave me lessons
He gave me purpose, I traded my ways, and never looked back for a minute
All done through love, I'll never forget it
Prayed two hours a day, I was getting better
Reading, skillful, and fluent in speaking with the Creator
My faith prepared me to deal with no limitations
I am a game changer
If you want to be a game changer, pray the next poem
It will change your life

Salvation

Lord Jesus, I accept You fully into my life. I believe You died on the cross for my sins, and I repent of every wrong that I have committed. Take over my life and save my soul. Make me whole in Your name. Use me for Your purpose. For I will forever glorify Your name. In Jesus's name I pray.

Amen, amen, amen.

You are now a game changer, royalty.

Go make history!

Lightning Source UK Ltd.
Milton Keynes UK
UKHW010840160421
382096UK00001B/84